THE BANK

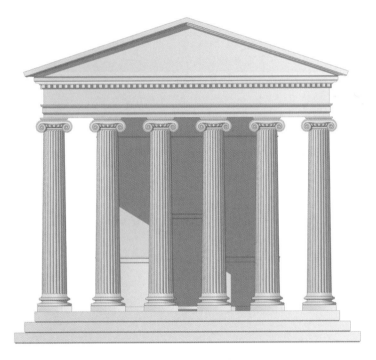

David and Patricia Armentrout

Rourke

Publishing LLC

Vero Beach, Florida 32964

www.rourkepublishing.com

PHOTO CREDITS: © Francis Twitty: cover; © Melissa Carroll: page 5; © Frances Twitty: page 6; © Yvonne Chamberlain: page 8; © Rick Rhay: page 9; © Jim Parkin: page 10; © Paolo Florendo: page 11; © Tomaz Levstek: page 15; © Roberta Osborne: page 17; © Rarpia: page 18; © Blaney Photo: page 19; © Sean Locke: page 20; © Talk Kienas: page 21; © Milan Radulovic: page 22

Edited by Kelli Hicks

Cover design by Teri Intzegian
Interior design by Teri Intzegian

Library of Congress Cataloging-in-Publication Data

Armentrout, David, 1962-
 The bank / David and Patricia Armentrout.
     p. cm. -- (Our community)

 ISBN 978-1-60472-335-9
 1. Banks and banking--Juvenile literature. I. Armentrout, Patricia, 1960- II.

Title.
 HG1609.A76 2009
 332.1--dc22

2008016343

Printed in the USA

CG/CG

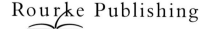

Rourke Publishing

www.rourkepublishing.com – rourke@rourkepublishing.com
Post Office Box 3328, Vero Beach, FL 32964

Table of Contents

What is a Bank?

A bank is a **safe place to keep money.** Do you have a bank at home?

A bank can hold **allowance** money, or money you earn from doing jobs around the house.

A bank is a business in your community that holds more than one person's money.

A bank will count all the coins in your piggy bank for you.

Banks help people and companies manage money and do business.

Deposits and Withdrawals

A bank **account** can help you manage your money. Money you put in an account is a **deposit**.

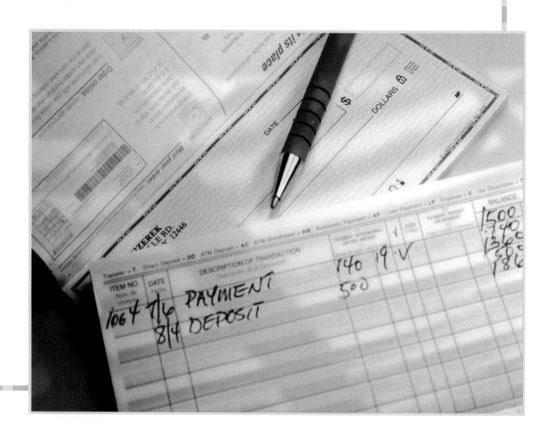

Money you take out is
a **withdrawal.**

Checking Account

A checking account allows you to pay for things without using cash. After you deposit money into the account, you can use a check to buy things, or to pay bills.

Signing a check gives your bank permission to take money from your account.

Many people use checks to pay bills through the mail.

Savings Account

You can save money with a savings account. A savings account can also earn money. Banks borrow money from savings accounts and pay account holders **interest**.

What are you saving your
money to buy?

Bank Business

Banks make money like other businesses. Banks loan money and charge the borrower a fee. This fee is also called interest.

Banks loan money for big purchases like cars and houses.

A bank manager helps a customer with a loan.

Bank Security

Banks use cameras, guards, and alarms to stop thieves. A vault keeps money safe. A vault is a secure room with thick walls and a heavy steel door.

Safe Deposit Boxes

Safe deposit boxes line the walls inside the vault. Customers use them to store important papers and other valuables safely.

Banks charge a fee to rent a safe deposit box.

ATM

Everyone likes to do things easily. An ATM, or automated teller machine, is easy to use. You can quickly withdraw cash from your bank account using an ATM.

ATMs are at banks and other places
where people need them most, grocery
stores and shopping malls.

Communities Need Banks

Banks are an important business in every community. Banks help people manage money, and keep valuables safe.

A bank customer makes a deposit.

Glossary

account (uh-KOUNT): a record of money

allowance (uh-LOU-uhns): money received
  on a regular basis

deposit (di-POZ-it): adding or putting in

interest (IN-trist): the cost of borrowing money

withdrawal (with-DRAW-uhl): taken away
  or removed

INDEX

FURTHER READING

Hammonds, Heather. *Banking.* Smart Apple Media, 2006.

Meachen, Dana. *What is a Bank?* Gareth Stevens Audio, 2005.

Roberson, Erin. *All About Money.* Children's Press, 2005.

WEBSITES

www.bankingkids.com
www.treas.gov/kids

ABOUT THE AUTHORS

David and Patricia Armentrout specialize in nonfiction children's books. They enjoy exploring different topics and have written about many subjects, including sports, animals, history, and people. David and Patricia love to spend their free time outdoors with their two boys and dog Max.